GALATIANS

WHY GOD
ACCEPTS US

JACK
KUHATSCHEK

11 STUDIES
FOR INDIVIDUALS
OR GROUPS

Life
Builder
Study

INTER-VARSITY PRESS
36 Causton Street, London SW1P 4ST, England
Email: ivp@ivpbooks.com
Website: www.ivpbooks.com

Originally published in the United States of America in the LifeGuide® Bible Studies series
in 2000 by InterVarsity Press, Downers Grove, Illinois
First published in Great Britain by Scripture Union in 2000
This edition published in Great Britain by Inter-Varsity Press 2018

British Library Cataloguing-in-Publication Data
A catalogue record for this book is available from the British Library.

ISBN: 978-1-78359-806-9

Printed in Great Britain by Ashford Colour Ltd, Gosport, Hampshire

Inter-Varsity Press publishes Christian books that are true to the Bible and that communicate
the gospel, develop discipleship and strengthen the church for its mission in the world.

IVP originated within the Inter-Varsity Fellowship, now the Universities and Colleges Christian
Fellowship, a student movement connecting Christian Unions in universities and colleges
throughout Great Britain, and a member movement of the International Fellowship of
Evangelical Students. Website: www.uccf.org.uk. That historic association is maintained,
and all senior IVP staff and committee members subscribe to the UCCF Basis of Faith.

Contents

Getting the Most Out of *Galatians*

We all want to be accepted—by our family, by our friends and most of all by God. But so often people accept us only *if* we are attractive, smart, wealthy or powerful. So we work hard to project the right image and to conceal our faults.

We often transfer this attitude to our relationship with God. We feel we must earn his acceptance. If we could only work harder, live better, pray longer, witness to more people—then we might get on God's good side.

In Galatians Paul challenges this kind of thinking. He says it's futile to try to earn God's acceptance when we are already accepted in Christ. His message frees us from living out of a sense of guilt. We find fresh assurance of God's love and renewed power to serve him.

Galatians was written by Paul sometime between A.D. 48-49. It was probably addressed to the churches in Antioch, Iconium, Lystra and Derbe, which were located in the Roman province of Galatia. Paul and Barnabas visited these cities during their first missionary journey. Their reception was unforgettable. Acts 13—14 tells us they were driven out of Antioch, they fled from Iconium, and Paul was stoned in Lystra! Yet in spite of the opposition against Paul and Barnabas, people believed the gospel and churches were formed.

The real threat arose shortly thereafter. Certain people infiltrated the new churches with a different message. "Paul omitted an important part of the gospel," they claimed. "You must also be circumcised and keep the law of Moses if you want to be saved" (see Acts 15:1). Their arguments were impressive and their religious zeal was undeniable. The Galatians were almost persuaded when Paul received word of what was happening. Quickly he dictated this letter and sent it to be read in each of the churches. Centuries later it still radiates the heat of Paul's anger. These preachers were impostors. Their gospel was perverted. The Galatians were in grave danger!

This study guide introduces you to the most passionate and forceful letter in the New Testament. The guide consists of eleven forty-five minute studies which allow you to interact with and apply the main idea in each passage. In the final study the "Now or Later" section provides questions to help you review the letter. You also grapple with some contemporary issues which are related to those problems faced by Paul and the Galatians. You may want to make this a separate session of study.

Suggestions for Individual Study

1. As you begin each study, pray that God will speak to you through his Word.

2. Read the introduction to the study and respond to the personal reflection question or exercise. This is designed to help you focus on God and on the theme of the study.

3. Each study deals with a particular passage—so that you can delve into the author's meaning in that context. Read and reread the passage to be studied. If you are studying a book, it will be helpful to read through the entire book prior to the first study. The questions are written using the language of the New International Version, so you may wish to use that version of the Bible. The New Revised Standard Version is also recommended.

4. This is an inductive Bible study, designed to help you discover for yourself what Scripture is saying. The study includes three types of questions. *Observation* questions ask about the basic facts: who, what, when, where and how. *Interpretation* questions delve into the meaning of the passage. *Application* questions help you discover the implications of the text for growing in Christ. These three keys unlock the treasures of Scripture.

Write your answers to the questions in the spaces provided or in a personal journal. Writing can bring clarity and deeper understanding of yourself and of God's Word.

5. It might be good to have a Bible dictionary handy. Use it to look up any unfamiliar words, names or places.

6. Use the prayer suggestion to guide you in thanking God for what you have learned and to pray about the applications that have come to mind.

7. You may want to go on to the suggestion under "Now or Later," or you may want to use that idea for your next study.

Suggestions for Members of a Group Study

1. Come to the study prepared. Follow the suggestions for individual study mentioned above. You will find that careful preparation will greatly enrich your time spent in group discussion.

2. Be willing to participate in the discussion. The leader of your group will not be lecturing. Instead, he or she will be encouraging the members of the group to discuss what they have learned. The leader will be asking the questions that are found in this guide.

3. Stick to the topic being discussed. Your answers should be based on the verses which are the focus of the discussion and not on outside authorities such as commentaries or speakers. These studies focus on a particular passage of Scripture. Only rarely should you refer to other portions of the Bible. This allows for everyone to participate in in-depth study on equal ground.

4. Be sensitive to the other members of the group. Listen attentively when they describe what they have learned. You may be surprised by their insights! Each question assumes a variety of answers. Many questions do not have "right" answers, particularly questions that aim at meaning or application. Instead the questions push us to explore the passage more thoroughly.

When possible, link what you say to the comments of others. Also, be affirming whenever you can. This will encourage some of the more hesitant members of the group to participate.

5. Be careful not to dominate the discussion. We are sometimes so eager to express our thoughts that we leave too little opportunity for others to respond. By all means participate! But allow others to also.

6. Expect God to teach you through the passage being discussed and through the other members of the group. Pray that you will have an enjoyable and profitable time together, but also that as a result of the study you will find ways that you can take action individually and/or as a group.

7. Remember that anything said in the group is considered confidential and should not be discussed outside the group unless specific permission is given to do so.

8. If you are the group leader, you will find additional suggestions at the back of the guide.

1

Good &
Bad News

You may see them on television preaching a gospel of prosperity. Or they may knock on your door, offering you a free magazine and inviting you to discuss their beliefs. They may even claim to have their own scriptures that record new revelation from God. The church has always been plagued by false teachers, heretics and followers of various cults. Usually such people have an aggressive program for winning new converts.

GROUP DISCUSSION. If a close Christian friend of yours was almost persuaded to join a cult, how would you respond?

PERSONAL REFLECTION. When members of a cult knock on your door and invite you to talk about their beliefs, what do you usually do, and why?

How are we to respond to those who preach or accept a twisted gospel? Paul gives us an example in this passage.

The letter to the Galatians begins abruptly. After the salutation in verses 1-5, Paul omits the customary expression of thanksgiving we find in his letters to the Ephesians, Philippians, Colossians and others. Instead, he plunges immediately into an impassioned discussion of some astonishing news he has heard about the Galatians. *Read Galatians 1:1-10.*

1. How would you describe the mood of this passage?

2. The word *apostle* means "one who is sent." Paul specifies that he is sent by God, not people, in verse 1. Why would he be concerned about this distinction?

3. In three brief verses (3-5) Paul tells us an enormous amount about the gospel. What do we learn?

4. Which aspect of the gospel do you especially need now? Explain.

5. In verses 6-7 Paul summarizes the problem that caused him to write this letter. What was happening in the Galatian churches?

6. Verse 6 implies that if we desert the gospel we also desert God. Why would this be true?

7. Why do you think Paul is so harsh in his judgment of those who preach a different gospel (vv. 8-9)?

_____

8. How might the way we present the gospel be different if we were seeking the approval of people instead of God (v. 10)?

_____

9. What are some ways the gospel is being perverted today?

_____

10. According to this passage, how can we ensure that the gospel we believe and preach is the true gospel?

_____

11. What can you do to increase your understanding of the gospel?

Confess before God the ways in which you are seeking the approval of others before him. Ask God to help you turn your priorities around.

Now or Later

Visit your local Christian bookstore this week and look through various books they offer on cults and new religions to get specific examples of the ways the gospel is being perverted today.

2

Why Believe
the Gospel?

Have you ever been talking with someone about the gospel when suddenly he or she says, "But that's just *your* opinion!"? This raises an important question. If the gospel is merely our opinion, then why should anyone listen to us? There are many other religions in the world, each one claiming to be a path to God. Who are we to assert that the gospel is the only true message of salvation?

GROUP DISCUSSION. What is the primary reason why you believe the gospel is true and not just a nice story?

PERSONAL REFLECTION. Think back on the events surrounding your own conversion to Christianity. Were you influenced more by intellectual arguments, the evidence of changed lives or something else? Explain.

Paul's opponents questioned the authenticity of the gospel he preached. In this passage he sets out to describe and defend the source of his gospel. In so doing he tells us why the gospel message is unique. *Read Galatians 1:11—2:10.*

1. In 1:11-12 Paul claims he received the gospel from Jesus Christ, not people. How does his brief autobiography in 1:13-24 confirm this claim?

---

2. Imagine being in Paul's position. What would it be like to receive the gospel directly from God?

---

3. What practical difference would it make to the Galatians whether Paul received his gospel from people or from God?

---

4. Paul obviously did not need human authorization to preach the gospel. Why then did he present his gospel to the leaders in Jerusalem (2:1-2)?

---

5. Why was it significant that Titus (a Gentile) was not compelled to be circumcised (the sign of becoming a Jew, 2:3-5)?

---

6. Paul refused to give in to false teachers on the matter of circumcision "so that the truth of the gospel might remain with you" (2:5). How do you show your concern to preserve the gospel?

7. How did the leaders in Jerusalem respond to Paul's message and ministry (2:6-10)?

Why was their endorsement of Paul's gospel and ministry important both then and now?

---

8. The apostles were not simply zealous to preserve the gospel. They also felt called to proclaim the gospel (2:7-10). Who do you feel called to go to with the gospel?

---

9. What steps can you take this week to bring the good news to someone?

---

10. How can Paul's testimony in this passage increase your confidence in the truth of the gospel?

Ask God to help you be a bearer of the good news.

Now or Later

Make a list of three or four non-Christian friends you know in your neighborhood, at work or at school. Begin praying for them regularly, asking God to open their hearts to the gospel.

3

Accepting
Others

Galatians 2:11-21

Have you ever felt like avoiding certain types of Christians? Perhaps you don't like their theology. You may disapprove of their lifestyle. Or you may prefer to avoid people of their race, nationality or economic background. Frank S. Mead's *Handbook of Denominations in the United States* lists over two hundred denominations and subgroups—many of which have fought, divided, and subdivided to avoid those who don't meet their standards.

GROUP DISCUSSION. What types or groups of Christians do you feel like avoiding? Why?

PERSONAL REFLECTION. What difficulties have you had with relating to Christian friends or acquaintances whose beliefs are different from yours? If it seems appropriate, take time to confess your biases to God before you begin the study.

In this passage Paul helps us see why our failure to accept other

Christians can conflict with the basic message of the gospel. *Read Galatians 2:11-21.*

---

1. How were Peter and the other Jews not "acting in line with the truth of the gospel" (vv. 11-14)?

---

2. How might their actions have forced "Gentiles to follow Jewish customs" (v. 14)?

---

3. What nonessential customs do Christians sometimes force on each other?

Which of these are you most likely to be concerned about and why?

---

4. Why is it wrong to make such customs a basis for fellowship (vv. 15-16)?

---

5. To *justify* (vv. 15-17) is a legal term meaning the person on trial is declared not guilty and deserves all the privileges of one who has not broken the law. How might justification by faith lead some to claim that "Christ promotes sin" (v. 17)?

6. How does Paul refute the accusation that Christ promotes sin (vv. 17-19)?

7. How has Christ enabled us to die to the law and to live for God (v. 20)?

8. Practically speaking, what does it mean to live for God?

9. If we have died to the law as a means of being accepted by God, how should this affect the way we approach God?

10. How should God's acceptance of us affect our attitude toward other Christians—even those from different races, backgrounds and traditions?

Pray for discernment about your own attitudes toward others, asking God to make you more accepting.

Now or Later

Write down two or three different Christian groups you tend to avoid or disapprove of. Do your feelings and reasons for avoiding these people conflict with Paul's message in this passage? If so, ask God to help you to accept those he has accepted in Christ.

4

Why God Accepts Us

We all want to be accepted. We do everything we can to win people's approval and avoid their rejection. But if we work so hard to please people, then what about God? How can we possibly meet his perfect standards?

GROUP DISCUSSION. Why do you think Christians often have a hard time believing that God accepts them unconditionally in Christ?

PERSONAL REFLECTION. Do you ever feel unacceptable to God? Explain why.

The Galatians felt these inner struggles. They wanted to be fully accepted by God. But they seemed to forget that God had already accepted them. They also forgot *why*. In fact, their thinking became so mixed up that Paul wondered whether they had been bewitched! In 3:1-14 Paul sets out to break the "spell" the Galatians are under by asking five pointed questions and examining six key Old Testament passages. *Read Galatians 3:1-14.*

1. From verses 1-5 try to reconstruct in chronological order the Galatians' spiritual pilgrimage.

2. In what ways did the Galatians' behavior seem "bewitched" and "foolish" according to verses 1-5?

3. In what ways do we sometimes try to earn God's favor by what we do?

4. How can a vivid understanding of Christ's crucifixion (v. 1) guard us from thinking we must earn God's favor?

5. When we follow the example of Abraham's faith, what are the results (vv. 6-9)?

6. How does Abraham's experience contrast with that of the person who seeks to earn God's acceptance (vv. 10-12)?

7. The word *redeemed* means to deliver from some evil by paying a price. How and why did Christ redeem us (v. 13-14)?

---

8. How does the gift of the Spirit affirm that God accepts us completely in Christ?

---

9. How have you been blessed by the Spirit's presence in your life?

There are several key words in verses 1-14 that describe what Christ has done for us. Identify some of these, then spend time thanking God for each one.

Now or Later

Take a piece of paper and draw a line down the middle. On the left side write down some of the reasons why you feel unacceptable to God. On the right side write what this passage says about why God accepts us. How should the reasons in the right column help you to think and feel differently about what you wrote in the left column?

5

Exposing Our Needs

Galatians 3:15-29

"Honey," Jill calls out, "you'd better call the repairman. Our TV is on the blink again."

"Who needs a repairman!" Ron replies confidently. "I can fix it myself."

Four hours later. "There, that should do it." As Ron plugs it in, there's a loud buzzing noise, smoke rises from the TV, the lights begin to flicker, and then darkness blacks out the room.

"Uh . . . maybe you're right, dear," Ron says sheepishly. "I suppose calling a repairman couldn't hurt."

GROUP DISCUSSION. Why is admitting we have a problem often so difficult for us?

PERSONAL REFLECTION. What problem have you had difficulty admitting to yourself and others?

People must admit they need help before they can receive it. Yet often this is very difficult. In Galatians 3:15-29 Paul tells us how God exposes our need for Christ. *Read Galatians 3:15-29.*

1. What key statements does Paul make in this passage about the law and God's promises?

---

2. Why is the law unable to set aside or add to the promises spoken to Abraham (vv. 15-18)?

---

3. If the law did not set aside or add to the promises given to Abraham, then why was it given (vv. 19-25)?

---

4. What evidence do you see in the media that "the whole world is a prisoner of sin" (v. 22)?

---

5. How does a clear grasp of God's law help us to realize our need for Christ (vv. 22-25)?

---

6. How then should a knowledge of the law's purpose affect our evangelism?

7. In verse 28 Paul lists several ways in which people have been catego-
rized. How have these categories sometimes functioned as barriers?

8. In light of the context, how have these barriers been broken down
in Christ?

9. In what practical ways should this affect our relationships with
the groups mentioned in verse 28?

10. Jesus once told a Pharisee that a person who is forgiven little
loves little but a person who is forgiven much loves much (Luke
7:36-50). How has a knowledge of your former condition increased
your love and appreciation for Christ?

*Ask God to help you put aside your pride and expose your needs to him
and to your Christian friends and family. Ask him to allow your aware-
ness of your need for him to prompt you to reach out to others.*

Now or Later

Paul says that in Christ the barriers between races ("neither Jew nor
Greek"), social classes ("slave nor free"), and sexes ("male nor
female") have been broken down. What evidence do you still see of
these barriers in your own church or the church at large? What factors have hindered the true unity that is ours in Christ?

6

The Joys of Growing Up

Galatians 4:1-20

In James Barrie's book *Peter Pan*, he describes a place called Never-Never Land, where children never grow up. To get there you must "take the second star to the right and go straight on till morning."

Have you ever longed to be a child again—to be free from work, mortgage payments, bills and taxes? Remember the carefree days, when from morning till night your job was to play?

GROUP DISCUSSION. If you could be a child again for one week, what age would you pick, and why?

PERSONAL REFLECTION. What are some of the things you miss most about being a child?

Yet aren't we forgetting something? Just think of all the things we *couldn't* do as children. The Galatians longed to return to the spiritual childhood of the law, but in this passage Paul reminds them—and us—of the joys of growing up. *Read Galatians 4:1-20.*

1. In what ways does Paul shatter the Galatians' illusions about spiritual childhood?

2. In verses 1-2 Paul refers to practices in Roman society. How was a Roman child no different from a slave?

3. How was life under the law like spiritual childhood (vv. 3-7)?

4. Verse 4 states, "When the time had fully come, God sent his Son." How did things change because of his coming (vv. 4-7)?

5. God has also sent the Spirit of his Son into our hearts, calling out, "*Abba* Father" (v. 6). In what ways have you experienced an intimate relationship with the Father?

6. In view of Paul's discussion in verses 1-7, how does the Galatians' behavior seem incredible (vv. 8-11)?

7. In what ways do you sometimes act like a spiritual slave?

How can you begin acting more like God's beloved son or daughter?

---

8. How and why had the Galatians' attitude toward Paul changed (vv. 12-20)?

---

9. What do these verses reveal about Paul's feelings toward the Galatians?

---

10. How do verses 12-20 illustrate the care and concern we should have for other members of God's family?

Spend a few minutes of intimate prayer with the Father, thanking him for the privileges of being a member of his family.

Now or Later

Because we are members of God's family, Paul says, "God sent the Spirit of his Son into our hearts, the Spirit who calls out, 'Abba, Father.'" Abba is an expression of intimacy between a parent and a son or daughter—much like saying "dearest Father." To what extent do you feel that kind of intimacy with your heavenly Father? Pray that the Holy Spirit will help you realize how close you are to the heart of God.

7

Do-It-Yourself Religion

Trusting God can seem risky. What if he lets us down? Still worse, what if our faith is simply foolishness? When such thoughts enter our minds, it's easy to panic. We are tempted to take back what we have entrusted to God. We feel safer taking matters into our own hands.

GROUP DISCUSSION. Why are we often uncomfortable in situations where we aren't in control (for example, a roller coaster, a sickness and so on)?

PERSONAL REFLECTION. In what kinds of situations do you find it most difficult to trust God? Why?

Abraham struggled to trust God while waiting for God's promise of a son. He rushed God's plan and had a son through his slave Hagar. Later, even though he and Sarah were very old, the promised son was born. This story, which Paul draws on in Galatians, has become a timeless illustration of do-it-yourself religion versus trust in the promises of God. Brace yourself! We will be introduced to women who are compared to covenants, mountains and even cities. *Read Galatians 4:21—5:1.*

---

1. This passage is filled with contrasts between people, places and ways of life. What contrasts do you see in 4:21—5:1?

---

2. How were Abraham's two sons (Ishmael and Isaac) different according to 4:21-23?

---

3. What does Paul mean when he says that the son of the slave woman was born the "ordinary way," but the son of the free woman was "the result of a promise" (4:23; see also 4:29)?

---

4. In 4:24 Paul says that the story of Hagar and Sarah may be understood "figuratively" (NIV) or "allegorically" (NASB). What do Hagar, the covenant from Sinai and "the present city of Jerusalem" have in common (4:24-25)?

---

5. How is Sarah (who, although unnamed, is the other woman in the story) similar to the new covenant and to the Jerusalem that is above (4:26-27)?

6. How do the two sons, two covenants and two cities illustrate two radically different views we can have about salvation?

7. Paul states that just as Ishmael persecuted Isaac, so too those born the ordinary way still persecute those born by the power of the Spirit (4:29). How have you seen this to be true, even in your own life?

8. How does Paul describe the ultimate fate of the slave woman's and the free woman's spiritual descendants (4:30)?

9. The spiritual principle described in this passage has broad application. Throughout Scripture God promises to accomplish that which we cannot do on our own. Think of Abraham, Moses, Joshua, Gideon, the apostles and others. In what areas are you trusting in the promises of God and the power of the Spirit to accomplish the extraordinary?

10. In 5:1 Paul states that Christ set us free so that we could experience freedom! Given the thrust of Galatians 1—4, what does Paul mean when he says we are free?

11. What are some present-day threats to our spiritual freedom?

What are some practical ways we can "stand firm" against them?

Ask God to help you stand against any threat to spiritual freedom in society and in your life.

Now or Later

John Stott writes:

> The persecution of the true church is not always by the world, who are strangers unrelated to us, but by our half-brothers, religious people, the nominal church. It has always been so. The Lord Jesus was bitterly opposed, rejected, mocked and condemned by His own nation. The fiercest opponents of the apostle Paul, who dogged his footsteps and stirred up strife against him, were the official church, the Jews. . . . And the greatest enemies of the evangelical faith today are not unbelievers, who when they hear the gospel often embrace it, but the church, the establishment, the hierarchy. (*The Message of Galatians* [IVP, 1992], p. 127)

Why do you think religious people are often the greatest enemies of Christians?

8

Severe
Warning

Galatians 5:2-12

"Help!" the man cried as he dangled helplessly from the edge of a cliff. Can anyone up there help me?"

"Yes," answered a heavenly voice, "I'll help you. But first you must let go."

"Let go!" gasped the man. "But then I'd fall!"

"I'll catch you," replied the voice.

There was a long pause, then the man cried out, "Can anyone *else* up there help me?"

If we want Christ to save us, then we must let go of the idea that we can save ourselves—even a little.

GROUP DISCUSSION. If you were the man hanging from the cliff in the story, would you have let go? Why or why not?

PERSONAL REFLECTION. Do you find it difficult to trust Christ alone for your salvation? Why?

Up to this point Paul has passionately argued for justification by faith in Christ. He has also ruthlessly demonstrated the futility of seeking righteousness by the law. Now the Galatians must decide between law or grace—they *cannot* have both. *Read Galatians 5:2-12.*

---

1. Picture Paul writing verses 2-12. What can you discover about his mood from these verses?

---

2. In your own words explain the consequences of trying to be justified by law (vv. 2-4).

---

3. Paul's warning probably surprised the Galatians. They knew faith in Christ was *necessary* for their salvation; they simply wondered whether it was *sufficient.* Why does any attempt to earn God's acceptance destroy justification by faith?

---

4. In verses 2-4 Paul gave stern warnings to those who desired to be circumcised. Now he says, "neither circumcision nor uncircumcision has any value" (v. 6). How can both of these views be true?

---

5. In verse 6 we might have expected Paul to say, "The only thing that counts is faith." How does his actual statement give us a balanced view of the Christian life?

---

6. Give examples of how you might express your faith through loving acts.

7. Paul compares the Galatians to runners in a race and to a batch of dough (vv. 7-9). How do these comparisons illustrate the nature and perils of the Christian life?

8. Considering the seriousness of the threat facing the Galatians, how would you explain Paul's confident statement in the first half of verse 10?

9. In verses 10-12 Paul makes some severe statements about those who are troubling the Galatians (especially v. 12!). Even by today's standards they are harsh. Why was he so upset?

10. In Paul's day the cross was offensive (v. 11) because it declared that circumcision and law-keeping were unnecessary for justification. Why is the cross offensive today?

11. How can you encourage someone you know to stay in the race?

Ask God to help you to be both a good runner and companion in the race.

Now or Later

In our culture we are hesitant to warn someone who is in moral or spiritual danger. Why do you think that is so? How can you develop a "tough love" with those who face these dangers?

9

Living by the Spirit

Galatians 5:13-26

In William Golding's book *Lord of the Flies,* a plane carrying a group of schoolboys crashes, killing the pilot, and the boys are left without supervision on a remote island in the Pacific. At first they try to maintain order and discipline, so they elect a leader named Ralph. But in the absence of moral restraints, many of the schoolboys eventually become savages and even murderers. At the conclusion of the book Ralph is running for his life from the boys, who plan to kill him and put his head on a stake. At the last moment, he runs out of the jungle and is saved by a naval officer, who is astonished at the transformation in the schoolboys.

GROUP DISCUSSION. Imagine that all civil and criminal laws were abolished in your community. How and why might this affect the people who live there?

PERSONAL REFLECTION. Have you ever found yourself abusing your freedom in Christ since you know you can always ask for forgiveness later? Examine your conscience before God.

In Galatians 5 Paul explains the true meaning of Christian freedom. Then he describes how our lives can be transformed by God's Spirit. *Read Galatians 5:13-26.*

---

1. How would you summarize the radically different lifestyles Paul describes in this passage?

---

2. What is the difference between the two concepts of freedom described in verses 13-14?

---

3. In verse 15 Paul accuses the Galatians of "biting and devouring each other." Where do you see these practices among Christians today?

How would Paul's exhortations in verses 13-14 provide a remedy to this type of conduct?

4. What does it mean to "live by the Spirit" (v. 16)?

5. If we live by the Spirit, what does Paul assure us will happen (vv. 16-17)?

6. How is being led by the Spirit different than living under law (v. 18)?

7. Why is it so easy to recognize the acts of the sinful nature (vv. 19-21)?

8. How can Paul's warning in verse 21 be reconciled with his emphasis on justification by faith?

9. Why is *fruit* a good description of the Spirit's work in us (vv. 22-23)?

---

10. In what ways do you see the Spirit's fruit ripening in your life?

What fruit would you like to cultivate more?

---

11. Paul assumes that even though all Christians live by the Spirit, we do not always keep in step with the Spirit (vv. 25-26). In what ways do you struggle to keep in step with the Spirit?

Spend time thanking God for the Spirit's work in your life. Pray for the Spirit's help in those areas where you feel out of step.

Now or Later

In John 15 Jesus describes himself as the true vine and his followers as branches. Take time to read and meditate on that passage. What new insights does it give you about bearing fruit?

10

The Law of Love

In his book *Love Beyond Reason* John Ortberg writes, "If grace is the one thing the church has to offer, if there is no wonder like the wonder of grace, why do we leave it so easily? Why is it that churches filled with people who say they have been saved by grace can become such ungracious people?"[1] The fruit of the Spirit are most clearly demonstrated in our relationships with others—especially those who need extra care and support. Love is the visible and practical measure of our spirituality.

GROUP DISCUSSION. It has been said that the church is the only army on earth that shoots its wounded. How do you respond to that statement?

PERSONAL REFLECTION. Think of an occasion when someone showed you special love during a time of need. What did you appreciate most about their actions and attitude?

---

[1]John Ortberg, *Love Beyond Reason* (Grand Rapids: Zondervan, 1998), p. 141.

In this passage Paul describes how we should relate to the family of believers and to all people. *Read Galatians 6:1-10.*

1. Identify the various relationships Paul has in view in these verses.

2. Describe how you might feel if you were "caught in a sin" (v. 1).

3. What guidelines does Paul offer for dealing with a person who is caught in a sin, and why is each important?

4. What types of burdens might Paul have had in mind in verse 2?

5. What are some ways you might help Christians you know to carry these burdens?

6. How does the law of Christ (v. 2) differ from the kind of law-keeping urged by Paul's opponents?

7. The sins or burdens of others can lead us to feel superior. How can proper methods of self-examination correct this attitude (vv. 3-5)?

8. The idea of a Christian teacher receiving remuneration (v. 6) might seem unspiritual to some. What are some practical reasons Paul may have commanded this?

9. Paul describes the principle of sowing and reaping in verses 7-8. One person has expanded these verses as follows:

Sow a thought, reap an act.
Sow an act, reap a habit.
Sow a habit, reap a character.
Sow a character, reap a destiny.

Do you think this is an accurate and helpful understanding of these verses? Explain why or why not.

10. What other application of the principle of sowing and reaping does Paul make in verses 9 and 10?

---

11. What are one or two new ways you could begin sowing to the Spirit personally?

in relationships with other Christians?

in relationships with non-Christians?

Ask God to help you "do good to all people."

Now or Later

Think of one person in your church who is carrying a special burden. What can you do this week to help that person? Ask God to enable you to demonstrate his love and grace.

11

Getting Motivated

Peer pressure can exert a powerful influence on us. The style of our clothes, the kind of music we listen to, our vocabulary, even the soft drinks we buy are affected by what others do and say. We are often tempted to change our behavior so others will accept us. But such approval can have a high price tag.

GROUP DISCUSSION. Why do you think people are so concerned about being accepted by their peers?

PERSONAL REFLECTION. When are you most tempted to seek the approval of others?

In this final passage Paul helps us to consider whose approval we desire most. Paul normally dictated his letters while another wrote them down. At this point, however, he asks for the pen and writes the final words of this book in large letters—probably for emphasis. Here we look into the heart of both Paul and his opponents. We find their motives are as different as their messages. *Read Galatians 6:11-18.*

---

1. As you look at this passage as a whole, what contrasts do you see between appearance versus reality?

2. What do verses 12-13 reveal about the motives of Paul's opponents?

---

3. How would urging others to be circumcised help them to achieve their goals?

---

4. The approval of others was most important to Paul's opponents (v. 12). In what situations are you tempted to hide your Christianity in order to "make a good impression outwardly"?

---

5. The cross was regarded with horror as an instrument of criminal death in Paul's day, yet it was Paul's ground for boasting (v. 14)! What does it mean to boast in the cross?

How does it differ from the boasting of Paul's opponents?

---

6. How should boasting in the cross affect our desire for the world's approval (v. 14)?

How will it affect the world's attitude toward us?

7. Why does the new creation have value in contrast to the worthlessness of circumcision or uncircumcision (v. 15)?

_____

8. In Paul's closing blessing and benediction he mentions peace, mercy and the grace of our Lord Jesus Christ (vv. 16, 18). Why do we need each of these when we follow the "rule" of verses 14-15?

_____

9. Two of the false accusations against Paul were that he tried to please people rather than God (1:10), and that he still preached circumcision (5:11). How does verse 17 provide a powerful refutation of these claims?

_____

10. Paul bore on his body the marks of Jesus (the evidence of faithful service). What are the "marks of Jesus" in your life?

_____

11. How can this passage help you to purify your motives and goals ?

Take time to evaluate your life—especially where you have allowed the opinions or approval of others to weaken your commitment to Christ. Ask God to help you to care more about his approval than the approval of others. Then look for situations this week when you can put this new attitude into practice.

Now or Later

The following questions will help you to review what you've learned from Galatians and apply it to problems we face today.

1. As you think back over the book of Galatians, what major themes come to mind? Briefly summarize Paul's position on each one.

2. How has the book of Galatians changed your thinking or behavior in significant ways?

3. Throughout this letter Paul has referred to "the gospel." From what he has said, what are the most important elements of the gospel?

4. What things must be excluded from any presentation of the gospel or any proper response to the gospel?

5. It is not uncommon for people to try to pit the teachings of Jesus against those of Paul. For example, one person has written: "Luther and Calvin, we know, looked to the book of Romans in the Bible for their primary inspiration. Were they, unknowingly, possessed more by the Spirit of St. Paul than by the Spirit of Jesus Christ? Are we not on safer grounds if we look to our Lord's words to launch our reformation?" How would Paul have responded to this statement?

6. Critique the following in light of what you have learned in Galatians: "What must I do to be justified? (a) I must believe in Jesus Christ and thereby receive the forgiveness he offers through his death on the cross. (b) I must be baptized. (c) I must seek to obey the commandments of God with the help of his Spirit. If I faithfully do all of these, then God will accept me into his eternal kingdom." Is this a true or perverted statement of the gospel? Explain your answer.

7. Can someone be saved who firmly believes in a false or perverted gospel? Defend your position from what Paul has said in this letter.

8. Today many churches and Christian schools legislate rules for their members or students. These rules often oppose such practices as drinking alcoholic beverages, smoking, dancing, going to movies and so on. Those who make and enforce these rules are often criticized and labeled as "legalistic." Do you think this criticism is valid or invalid? Why?

9. What have you appreciated most about your study of Galatians?

Leader's Notes

Leading a Bible discussion can be an enjoyable and rewarding experience. But it can also be *scary*—especially if you've never done it before. If this is your feeling, you're in good company. When God asked Moses to lead the Israelites out of Egypt, he replied, "O Lord, please send someone else to do it"! (Ex 4:13). It was the same with Solomon, Jeremiah and Timothy, but God helped these people in spite of their weaknesses, and he will help you as well.

You don't need to be an expert on the Bible or a trained teacher to lead a Bible discussion. The idea behind these inductive studies is that the leader guides group members to discover for themselves what the Bible has to say. This method of learning will allow group members to remember much more of what is said than a lecture would.

These studies are designed to be led easily. As a matter of fact, the flow of questions through the passage from observation to interpretation to application is so natural that you may feel that the studies lead themselves. This study guide is also flexible. You can use it with a variety of groups—student, professional, neighborhood or church groups. Each study takes forty-five to sixty minutes in a group setting.

There are some important facts to know about group dynamics and encouraging discussion. The suggestions listed below should enable you to effectively and enjoyably fulfill your role as leader.

Preparing for the Study

1. Ask God to help you understand and apply the passage in your own life. Unless this happens, you will not be prepared to lead others. Pray too for the various members of the group. Ask God to open your hearts to the message of his Word and motivate you to action.

2. Read the introduction to the entire guide to get an overview of the entire book and the issues which will be explored.

3. As you begin each study, read and reread the assigned Bible passage to familiarize yourself with it.

4. This study guide is based on the New International Version of the Bible. It will help you and the group if you use this translation as the basis for your study and discussion.

5. Carefully work through each question in the study. Spend time in meditation and reflection as you consider how to respond.

6. Write your thoughts and responses in the space provided in the study guide. This will help you to express your understanding of the passage clearly.

7. It might help to have a Bible dictionary handy. Use it to look up any unfamiliar words, names or places. (For additional help on how to study a passage, see chapter five of *How to Lead a LifeBuilder Study*, IVP, 2018.)

8. Consider how you can apply the Scripture to your life. Remember that the group will follow your lead in responding to the studies. They will not go any deeper than you do.

9. Once you have finished your own study of the passage, familiarize yourself with the leader's notes for the study you are leading. These are designed to help you in several ways. First, they tell you the purpose the study guide author had in mind when writing the study. Take time to think through how the study questions work together to accomplish that purpose. Second, the notes provide you with additional background information or suggestions on group dynamics for various questions. This information can be useful when people have difficulty understanding or answering a question. Third, the leader's notes can alert you to potential problems you may encounter during the study.

10. If you wish to remind yourself of anything mentioned in the leader's notes, make a note to yourself below that question in the study.

Leading the Study

1. Begin the study on time. Open with prayer, asking God to help the group to understand and apply the passage.

2. Be sure that everyone in your group has a study guide. Encourage

the group to prepare beforehand for each discussion by reading the introduction to the guide and by working through the questions in the study.

3. At the beginning of your first time together, explain that these studies
are meant to be discussions, not lectures. Encourage the members of the
group to participate. However, do not put pressure on those who may be
hesitant to speak during the first few sessions. You may want to suggest the
following guidelines to your group.

❑ Stick to the topic being discussed.

❑ Your responses should be based on the verses which are the focus of
the discussion and not on outside authorities such as commentaries or
speakers.

❑ These studies focus on a particular passage of Scripture. Only rarely
should you refer to other portions of the Bible. This allows for everyone
to participate in in-depth study on equal ground.

❑ Anything said in the group is considered confidential and will not be
discussed outside the group unless specific permission is given to do so.

❑ We will listen attentively to each other and provide time for each person
present to talk.

❑ We will pray for each other.

4. Have a group member read the introduction at the beginning of the
discussion.

5. Every session begins with a group discussion question. The question or activity is meant to be used before the passage is read. The question
introduces the theme of the study and encourages group members to begin
to open up. Encourage as many members as possible to participate, and be
ready to get the discussion going with your own response.

This section is designed to reveal where our thoughts or feelings need to
be transformed by Scripture. That is why it is especially important not
to read the passage before the discussion question is asked. The passage
will tend to color the honest reactions people would otherwise give because
they are, of course, supposed to think the way the Bible does.

You may want to supplement the group discussion question with an
icebreaker to help people to get comfortable. See the community section of
the *Small Group Starter Kit* (IVP, 1995) for more ideas.

You also might want to use the personal reflection question with your
group. Either allow a time of silence for people to respond individually or

discuss it together.

6. Have a group member (or members if the passage is long) read aloud the passage to be studied. Then give people several minutes to read the passage again silently so that they can take it all in.

7. Question 1 will generally be an overview question designed to briefly survey the passage. Encourage the group to look at the whole passage, but try to avoid getting sidetracked by questions or issues that will be addressed later in the study.

8. As you ask the questions, keep in mind that they are designed to be used just as they are written. You may simply read them aloud. Or you may prefer to express them in your own words.

There may be times when it is appropriate to deviate from the study guide. For example, a question may have already been answered. If so, move on to the next question. Or someone may raise an important question not covered in the guide. Take time to discuss it, but try to keep the group from going off on tangents.

9. Avoid answering your own questions. If necessary, repeat or rephrase them until they are clearly understood. Or point out something you read in the leader's notes to clarify the context or meaning. An eager group quickly becomes passive and silent if they think the leader will do most of the talking.

10. Don't be afraid of silence. People may need time to think about the question before formulating their answers.

11. Don't be content with just one answer. Ask, "What do the rest of you think?" or "Anything else?" until several people have given answers to the question.

12. Acknowledge all contributions. Try to be affirming whenever possible. Never reject an answer. If it is clearly off-base, ask, "Which verse led you to that conclusion?" or again, "What do the rest of you think?"

13. Don't expect every answer to be addressed to you, even though this will probably happen at first. As group members become more at ease, they will begin to truly interact with each other. This is one sign of healthy discussion.

14. Don't be afraid of controversy. It can be very stimulating. If you don't resolve an issue completely, don't be frustrated. Move on and keep it in mind for later. A subsequent study may solve the problem.

15. Periodically summarize what the group has said about the passage. This helps to draw together the various ideas mentioned and gives continuity to the study. But don't preach.

16. At the end of the Bible discussion you may want to allow group members a time of quiet to work on an idea under "Now or Later." Then discuss what you experienced. Or you may want to encourage group members to work on these ideas between meetings. Give an opportunity during the session for people to talk about what they are learning.

17. Conclude your time together with conversational prayer, adapting the prayer suggestion at the end of the study to your group. Ask for God's help in following through on the commitments you've made.

18. End on time.

Many more suggestions and helps are found in *How to Lead a LifeBuilder Study*.

Components of Small Groups

A healthy small group should do more than study the Bible. There are four components to consider as you structure your time together.

Nurture. Small groups help us to grow in our knowledge and love of God. Bible study is the key to making this happen and is the foundation of your small group.

Community. Small groups are a great place to develop deep friendships with other Christians. Allow time for informal interaction before and after each study. Plan activities and games that will help you get to know each other. Spend time having fun together—going on a picnic or cooking dinner together.

Worship and prayer. Your study will be enhanced by spending time praising God together in prayer or song. Pray for each other's needs—and keep track of how God is answering prayer in your group. Ask God to help you to apply what you are learning in your study.

Outreach. Reaching out to others can be a practical way of applying what you are learning, and it will keep your group from becoming self-focused. Host a series of evangelistic discussions for your friends or neighbors. Clean up the yard of an elderly friend. Serve at a soup kitchen together, or spend a day working in the community.

Many more suggestions and helps in each of these areas are found

in the *Small Group Starter Kit*. You will also find information on
building a small group. Reading through the starter kit will be worth your
time.

Study 1. Galatians 1:1-10. Good & Bad News.
Purpose: To understand the importance of believing and preaching the
true gospel and the dangers associated with embracing a perverted
gospel.
General note. You may wish to begin the study by reading aloud the
introduction on pages 5-6 or by summarizing its content. If everyone has
read it prior to the study, you can briefly go over the main points.
Question 1. Encourage the group to look for words or phrases that express
the mood of the passage.
Question 2. "By adding the word 'apostle' Paul at once highlights his
claim to be commissioned by Jesus to preach the Gospel with authority
and to plant Christianity. It was this commission that was being challenged
by the Galatian legalizers. Greek-speaking Jews had used the word 'apostle'
for authorized representatives. With the coming of Christ, Christians
applied it to those commissioned by Christ as authoritative bearers of
the Gospel" (*Zondervan NIV Bible Commentary*, vol. 2, *New Testament*, eds.
Kenneth L. Barker & John Kohlenberger III [Grand Rapids: Zondervan,
1994], p. 708).

Someone may wonder what the difference is between "from men" and
"by man." "From men" would mean that Paul's commission was from a
human *only* and not from God. "By man" suggests that God appointed Paul
through the agency of humanity.

Let the group wrestle with this question. Don't be too quick to supply
the answer yourself since this tends to inhibit the discussion.
Questions 6-7. If discussion gets stuck on what the gospel is, remind the
group of their answers to question 3 concerning verses 3-5.

If someone asks about what Paul meant about being "eternally condemned" (vv. 8-9), you might be helped by John Stott, who writes: "The
Greek word twice translated 'eternally condemned' is *anathema*. It was
used in the Greek Old Testament for the divine ban, the curse of God
resting upon anything or anyone devoted by Him to destruction. The
story of Achan provides an example of this. . . . So the apostle Paul

desires that these false teachers should come under the divine ban, curse or *anathema*. That is, he expresses the wish that God's judgment will fall on them" (*The Message of Galatians* [Leicester: IVP, 1992], p. 24).

Question 8. Some may have questioned whether Paul changed his message to suit the audience in order to get the widest following wherever he went.

Question 9. It may not be wise at this point to expect detailed explanations of how the gospel is being perverted today. The issues involved should become clearer to members of your group as they study further in Galatians.

Study 2. Galatians 1:11—2:10. Why Believe the Gospel?

Purpose: To realize that the gospel Paul preached came from God, not humans.

Question 1. "Paul now proceeds to prove his claim. The proof seems to consist of two major parts. In the first place, he needs to give evidence for the claim itself (1:13-24): he must show that during the formative years of his ministry he did not receive training from the apostles. In the second place, he must deal with two subsequent events that probably had been used by the Judaizers as evidence against him (2:1-21)" (*New Bible Commentary: 21st Century Edition*, eds., G. J. Wenham et al. [Leicester: IVP, 1994], p. 1210).

Each incident Paul relates is intended in some way to prove that his gospel did not come from people but God. There are many other interesting facts about Paul's life in these verses, but be careful not to get sidetracked from the main points.

Notice that verse 11 echoes verse 1.

The visit to Jerusalem mentioned in 1:18-19 is probably the one described in Acts 9:26-30.

Question 2. See Acts 9:1-19 for the story of Paul's conversion.

Question 4. It seems likely that the visit to Jerusalem mentioned in 2:1-10 is the one recorded in Acts 11:29-30 (see also Acts 12:25). But no details are given in Acts about the events described in Galatians 2:1-10.

The revelation mentioned in 2:2 may have been the prophecy of Agabus recorded in Acts 11:27-28. However, the context of Galatians 2:1-10 suggests that God desired a meeting between Paul and the leaders in Jerusalem. Paul's gospel may have been independent of such men, but their endorsement would help to maintain the unity of the church and the continued purity of the gospel.

Paul's statement "for fear that I was running or had run my race in vain" probably didn't mean that he feared he had been preaching the wrong message. This would contradict everything he has said before. Without this meeting in Jerusalem, there are other ways in which Paul's ministry might have been in jeopardy. Urge your group to explore some of these other possibilities.

Question 5. Verses 3-5 give some specific statements about some of the issues that were at stake. Focus on these. If the discussion moves too far beyond these verses, remind people that the rest of the letter answers this question more fully.

Question 6. Martin Luther wrote, "We will suffer our goods to be taken away, our name, our life, and all we have; but the Gospel, our faith, Jesus Christ, we will never suffer to be wrested from us" (*Commentary on the Epistle to the Galatians* [Cambridge: James Clarke, 1953], p. 108).

Question 7. According to the *New Bible Commentary:*

> James, Peter and John showed him mutual respect and equality. Specifically, they *recognized* that God had given Paul a special apostolic gift to work among the Gentiles. There was some irony in this fact. Paul himself would not appeal to the Three as though he depended on their authority (that made no difference to the legitimacy of his ministry). The Judaizers, who had indeed appealed to that authority, however, turn out to be the ones violating the Jerusalem agreement by asking the Gentiles to be circumcised! (p. 1212)

Study 3. Galatians 2:11-21. Accepting Others.

Purpose: To realize that we must unconditionally accept other Christians because God has accepted us.

Questions 1-2. During the first century, Jews normally did not associate with Gentiles. However, Gentiles could become converts to Judaism by being circumcised and agreeing to obey the law (Ex 12:48-49; Num 15:14-16). Then it would be acceptable to have fellowship with them. The early church wrestled with the question of whether a gentile Christian must also become a Jew in order to be saved. The book of Galatians resulted from that controversy. *The New Bible Commentary* summarizes the situation as follows: "If the Christian Jew sat down to eat with the Gentiles, he would have been in danger of violating the ceremonial food laws. On the other hand, if he refused to eat with them, that behavior would have undermined the principle that Gentiles should be fully accepted as Christians without becoming Jews" (p. 1212).

Question 3. For example, consider certain ways of praying, certain dress at worship, certain lifestyle habits and so on.

Question 4. The incident with Peter becomes a springboard for a broader discussion of justification by faith (vv. 15-21). If God has accepted us unconditionally through Christ, then we must accept other Christians.

Question 5. If people have difficulty with this question, then ask, "If salvation isn't based on what *we* do but rather on what *Jesus* has done, then what's to prevent us from sinning? After all, we can always ask for forgiveness later." This issue will be covered more fully in study nine.

Questions 6-7. The group may have difficulty understanding verses 18-19. In verse 18 *what I destroyed* probably refers to Paul's trust in the law for justification. Paul knew he couldn't keep the law, so trying to "rebuild" his confidence in the law would be futile.

Don't allow the group to get bogged down on question 6. The main points to notice are that Paul emphatically denies that Christ promotes sin ("absolutely not," v. 17) and that Paul died to the law not in order to sin but rather "so that I might live for God" (v. 19).

In question 7 help the group to see that the demands of the law were fully satisfied when Christ was crucified. When Christ died then, spiritually speaking, we also died.

Question 8. Encourage group members to give examples from their own lives to flesh out the meaning of this question.

Study 4. Galatians 3:1-14. Why God Accepts Us.

Purpose: To realize that God accepts us not because of what *we* do but rather because of what *Christ* has done for us.

Question 1. This question should lead you to a broad understanding of what had happened to the Galatians between the time Paul first preached to them and the writing of this letter.

Question 2. There is a lot in these verses, so don't be satisfied with one or two answers. Paul asks five questions in verses 1-5, and each one points out something foolish in the Galatians' behavior.

This is the first time Paul mentions the Holy Spirit. He contrasts relying on the Spirit with relying on human effort (literally, "the flesh"). This contrast is picked up again and expanded later on in the letter.

Question 5. Paul stresses that faith is not a new concept—after all, Abraham believed. Likewise, faith does not conflict with God's original plans for Abraham, which envisioned worldwide blessing through faith in Christ.

Regarding verse 7, F. F. Bruce writes, "The Galatians were being urged [by the Judaizers] to become children of Abraham by adoption (since they were not his children by natural birth), and this, they were told, involved circumcision, just as it did for proselytes from paganism to Judaism. Paul maintains that, having believed the gospel and received God's gift of righteousness, they are Abraham's children already, in the only sense that matters in God's sight" (*Galatians*, p. 155).

Question 7. Christ redeemed us in order that we might receive the "blessing given to Abraham" and "the promises of the Spirit" (v. 14). Are these two purposes or one? Many commentators believe that verse 14 speaks of only one purpose of Christ's redemption. The two phrases "in order that" and "so that" are parallel in Greek (see also RSV) and may be two ways of describing the same thing—the first description being general and the second specific. If this view is correct, then the gift of the Spirit is the promised blessing.

Question 9. This is an important question. Help the group to see that God accepts us so completely that he comes to live within us through the Spirit.

Prayer. After studying this passage, words such as *crucified, Spirit, righteousness* and *blessing* should bring to mind a number of reasons for thanking and praising God for what he has done for us in Christ.

Study 5. Galatians 3:15-29. Exposing Our Needs.

Purpose: To realize God gave the law not to save us but to expose our need for Christ.

Question 2. Make sure the group focuses on how a human covenant is similar to God's covenant with Abraham. In verse 16 Paul says, "the promises were spoken to Abraham and to his seed." He probably has in mind several Old Testament passages, especially Genesis 22:18:

"Through your offspring [sometimes translated "seed"] all nations on earth will be blessed." The word *seed* in Hebrew, Greek and English is a collective singular and can refer to a single descendant or to many descendants. Paul claims that *seed* ultimately referred to Christ.

In verse 17 Paul says that the law was introduced 430 years after God's covenant with Abraham. Exodus 12:40 states that "the length of time the Israelite people lived in Egypt was 430 years." This verse would indicate that the period from Abraham to the giving of the law was longer than 430 years. However, the Samaritan Pentateuch and the Septuagint, a popular Greek translation of the New Testament, read: "The length of time the Israelite people lived in Egypt *and in Canaan* was 430 years." Paul may have been quoting from the Septuagint. Yet whatever the explanation, the number of years is peripheral to his argument. Therefore, if the issue arises, suggest that it might be better to discuss this after the study is over so your attention can focus on the main points.

Question 3. One purpose of the law was to be "in charge" of us and to have "supervision" over us (vv. 24-25). This supervisor, known as a pedagogue in Greek and Roman society, was a slave who was put in charge of a minor until he reached adulthood. Such slaves were often pictured with a rod or cane in their hands. A modern analogy would be a strict governess. John Stott writes: "Like a gaoler [the law] has thrown us into prison; like a *paidagōgos* it rebukes and punishes us for our misdeeds."

The group may wonder about the meaning of verse 20. It might interest you to know that more than three hundred different interpretations have been suggested for this verse! However, the living Bible may have captured its meaning: "God gave his laws to angels to give to Moses, who then gave them to the people; but when God gave his promise to Abraham, he did it by himself alone, without angels or Moses as go-betweens" (vv. 19-20). Paul's point is that the law is inferior to the promise because the former came indirectly and the latter directly.

Question 5. John Stott writes: "Not until the law has arrested and imprisoned us will we pine for Christ to set us free. Not until the law has condemned and killed us will we call upon Christ for justification and life. . . . Not until the law has humbled us even to hell will we turn to the gospel to raise us to heaven" (*Message of Galatians*, p. 93).

Question 8. Galatians 3:28 has been wrongly interpreted as teaching that *all* racial, social and sexual distinctions have been abolished in Christ. The Scriptures teach that there is God-given diversity within the body of Christ. We are all equal, but we are not all the same. Moisés Silva writes: "While this verse has been used and abused in the attempt to develop a Christian ethic, we cannot afford to ignore its great significance for the subject at hand. And especially in our day, when we have become very conscious of the destructive power of prejudice—whether based on ethnic identity, social standing, or gender—we should both rejoice in this gospel that countenances no spiritual preferences, and learn to conduct ourselves in a way that sets forth that truth before a confused world" (*The New Bible Commentary*, p. 1215).

Study 6. Galatians 4:1-20. The Joys of Growing Up.

Purpose: To realize some of our privileges as God's sons and daughters, especially when compared to the lives of those who were under the law.

Question 3. The group might notice that in verse 3 the Greek word *stoicheia* is translated "basic principles" by the NIV and "elemental spirits" by the RSV. At first glance there seems to be no logical connection between the two. But the relationship between them is actually quite simple.

The Greeks thought of the letters of the alphabet as the "elements" of words and sentences. They also thought of earth, water, air and fire as the elements of the material world, and they tended to deify these elements and worship them. Only the context can ultimately determine whether Paul intended the word *stoicheia* to be understood as *basic principles* (a reference to the law) or as *elemental spirits* (as used of Greek deities). In verses 8-9 he may have both meanings in mind.

You don't need to mention this if there are no questions about it in the group.

Question 4. John Stott helps us answer the question.

Why is the period of Christ's coming termed "the fulness of time"(AV)? Various factors combined to make it such. For instance, it was the time when Rome had conquered and subdued the known inhabited earth, when Roman roads had been built to facilitate travel and Roman legions had been stationed to guard them. It was also the time when the Greek language and culture had given a certain cohesion to society. At the same time, the old mythological gods of Greece and Rome were losing their hold on the common people, so that the hearts and minds of men everywhere were hungry for a religion that was real and satisfying. Further, it was the time when the law of Moses had done its work of preparing men for Christ, holding them under its tutelage and in its prison, so that they longed ardently for the freedom with which Christ could make them free. (*Message of Galatians*, pp. 105-6)

Question 6. There is nothing intrinsically wrong with "observing special days and months and seasons and years" (v. 10). Paul says in Romans 14 that Christians should follow their own consciences in such matters and not criticize others. These observances only become enslaving when we do them for the wrong reasons—believing that God will only accept us if do them.

Question 9. Paul's feelings are most clearly seen in his use of the metaphor of childbirth. Encourage your group to focus on the attitudes and feelings conveyed by this imagery.

Looking ahead to study 7. Some members of your group may not be familiar with the Old Testament account of Hagar and Sarah (Gen 15— 18; 21) which forms the basis for the next study. If this is so, you or some other member of your group should be prepared to *briefly* summarize the main aspects of the story before the next session. Of course the best preparation would be to have your group read these chapters before coming to the study. Suggest this at the end of study six.

Study 7. Galatians 4:21—5:1. Do-It-Yourself Religion.

Purpose: To consider how do-it-yourself religion differs from trust in the promises and power of God.

General note. Before you ask question 1, you may want to summarize the story of Sarah and Hagar (Gen 15-18, 21) or ask the group to do so based on the reading you asked them to do at the end of the last study.

Questions 2-3. Question 2 asks the group to *observe* the differences between Abraham's two sons. Question 3 asks them to *interpret* the meaning of these differences. If the group gives a full answer to question 2, then skip question 3.

Question 4. The kind of "allegory" Paul has in mind is known as typology. Typology has been defined as "a way of setting forth the biblical history of salvation so that some of its earlier phases [such as Hagar and Sarah] are seen as anticipations of later phases [such as the Old and New Covenants]" J. D. Douglas et al., eds., "Typology," *New Bible Dictionary*

2nd ed. [Wheaton, Ill.: Tyndale, 1982]).

Question 5. 4:27 is a quote from Isaiah 54:1. There the woman "who has a husband" refers to the city of Jerusalem before the Babylonian exile. It corresponds to Hagar. The "barren woman" refers to Jerusalem after the Babylonians have carried off her children and left her desolate. It corresponds to Sarah. God promises that after the exile Jerusalem will be rebuilt and restored to a position of unsurpassed glory. But Paul sees the ultimate fulfillment of the prophecy in the New Jerusalem, the eternal dwelling place of the people of God.

Question 6. As your group discusses the differences between salvation by faith and salvation by observing the law, be sure they also discuss how they are *illustrated* by the two sons (especially), two covenants and two cities.

Question 7. If your group still doesn't understand what Paul means by "born in the ordinary way," you might want to read them the following quote from James Montgomery Boice: "This contrast [between Ishmael and Isaac] lends itself well to the distinction Paul is trying to make between natural or man-made religion and supernatural or God-made religion. The religion of works and law corresponds to the natural birth of Ishmael; the religion of the Spirit, which is Christianity, corresponds to the supernatural birth of Isaac" (*Zondervan NIV Bible Commentary*, 2: 733).

Questions 10-11. The fact that 5:1 begins a new chapter obscures the fact that it is naturally linked to 4:31. When the two verses are read together, this becomes clearer.

Study 8. Galatians 5:2-12. Severe Warning.

Purpose: To understand the serious consequences of embracing a perverted gospel.

Question 1. This is perhaps the most severe warning in all of Paul's writings.

Question 2. Paul makes several disturbing statements. Chances are that someone in your group will feel personally or theologically threatened by what Paul is saying—especially with the warning "you have fallen away from grace."

It is natural for questions about the doctrine of eternal security to arise in people's minds when reading a passage such as this. But you might point out that Paul's major concern here is neither to confirm nor deny that doctrine. He is not raising the question "Are Christians eternally secure?" but rather "What are the consequences when a person embraces a perverted gospel?" Urge your group to seriously consider what Paul *is* saying rather than what he has left unsaid.

Nonetheless, what Paul is saying is so harsh that we are tempted to explain it away rather than truly explaining it. In the process a discussion of eternal security may be unavoidable. Therefore, consider the following.

Paul's statements should be allowed their full force. In the strongest possible language he states that if a person embraces a perverted gospel, he or she has no share in Christ or the grace that comes through him. In other words, no one can be saved by believing a false or perverted gospel.

But what about those who initially believe the true gospel but later on embrace a perverted gospel? Do they *lose* their salvation? This question is framed in such a way as to make a satisfactory answer impossible. If the answer is no, Paul's words are emptied of their force. If the answer is yes, the scriptural emphasis on eternal security is denied. Yet both must somehow be maintained. Perhaps a better question might be, Would a true Christian embrace a false gospel? The answer is found in a doctrine known as the perseverance of the saints.

Eternal security looks at the Christian from God's perspective. But the corollary of eternal security—perseverance of the saints—looks at the Christian from the human perspective. The same Scriptures which teach eternal security also teach that a true Christian will persevere, by the power and grace of God, unto the end (1 Jn 2:19). There will be many struggles, failures and successes. But the fight will be fought, the race completed and the battle won. From God's point of view the results are assured. Yet from our perspective we need constant strength, encouragement and even warnings—such as the one in this passage—to keep us on course.

Question 3. The Galatians felt that they must believe in Christ *and* be circumcised in order to be saved.

Question 7. As in 1 Corinthians 5:6-7, yeast in verse 9 is compared to a negative influence that starts small but eventually affects the whole. You might ask specifically how we "cut in on" one another while running the race.

Question 8. "I am confident in the Lord that you will take no other view." Even though this is a brief statement, it is very significant in this context. Is this merely a tactful way of expressing wishful thinking? Is it based on Paul's knowledge of the Galatians and his confidence in them? How can he possibly believe that they will not give in to his opponents when the threat seems so serious? Wrestle with these issues!

Study 9. Galatians 5:13-26. Living by the Spirit.

Purpose: To understand the true meaning of Christian freedom and how our lives can be transformed by the Spirit.

Question 4. The word *live* in verse 16 is a translation of the Greek word for *walk* (see NASB, RSV). It refers to our conduct, the manner in which we live.

The RSV translates the second half of verse 16 as a command: "and *do not* gratify the desire of the flesh" (my emphasis). The NIV translation ("you *will* not") is better. Paul strongly assures us that if we live by the Spirit we will not (and could not possibly) gratify the desires of the sinful nature.

Question 5. It is common to interpret verse 17 as though it were describing a frustrating conflict between the Spirit and our sinful nature which results in a spiritual deadlock.

The conflict is certainly real. If we seek to follow the desires of the sinful nature, the Spirit opposes us. Either way we face opposition! But if Paul is claiming that the conflict results in a spiritual deadlock, then he is contradicting rather than supporting the strong assurance he gave in verse 16. This means that it is essential for your group to keep from interpreting verse 17 in isolation. It was written to confirm and elaborate verse 16!

Question 6. The Spirit's leading in verse 18 has nothing to do with guidance (where we should live, who we should marry and so on). He is leading us toward moral and spiritual maturity.

Question 8. See comments on eternal security in leader's notes for study eight, question 2.

Question 11. The word for *live* in verse 25 is different from the word translated "live" in verse 16. The word in verse 25 refers to the Spirit as the source of our *life*. In verse 16 the word literally means "walk" (see note to question 4) and refers to the Spirit as the one who enables us to live differently as Christians. It stresses *conduct*. It would seem that all three expressions— walking by the Spirit (v. 16), being led by the Spirit (v. 18), and living by the Spirit (v. 25)—are closely related facets of the Spirit's ministry in us.

Study 10. Galatians 6:1-10. The Law of Love.

Purpose: To encourage us to build healthy and supportive relationships with other Christians and non-Christians.

Question 1. This question is designed to help your group to observe the basic structure of this passage and to give them a *brief* overview of what Paul is discussing.

Questions 2-3. Question 2 should give the members of your group a greater appreciation for Paul's guidelines for dealing with a person caught in a sin (question 3).

John Stott tells us that the Greek word translated "restore" (v. 1) "was used in secular Greek as a medical term for setting a fractured or dislocated bone. It is applied in Mark 1:19 to the apostles who were 'mending' their nets, although Arndt-Gingrich suggest a wider interpretation, namely that after a night's fishing, they were 'overhauling' (NEB) their nets 'by cleaning, mending, folding (them) together'" (*Message of Galatians*, p. 160).

Question 7. Someone in your group may wonder whether Paul's statement "each one should carry his own load" (v. 5) contradicts his command to "carry each other's burdens" (v. 2). Rather than giving your own answer to this question, ask that person (or the group) how he or she thinks the two statements can be reconciled. If they have difficulty answering this question, you might point out that there is a difference between the words "carry each other's *burdens*" and "carry his own *load*." The former has in mind any oppressive difficulty which a person is facing. The latter stresses that we are each responsible to God for our own attitudes and actions.

Question 9. The principle that you reap what you sow is very broad and has a number of applications. For example, Paul immediately applies it to sowing the sinful nature or the Spirit (v. 8). He also alludes to it when he talks about "doing good" (v. 9). But his discussion of the principle was probably prompted by the thought of Christians hoarding their money or squandering it rather than using it to help others—in this case those who teach them the Scriptures (see v. 6).

It is possible for verse 8 to be interpreted in such a way that it contradicts Paul's emphasis on justification by faith. Therefore, it might be helpful to ask your group how the two can be harmonized.

Question 11. It isn't necessary for everyone in the group to share how they intend to apply this principle. But even those who don't share should be encouraged to silently commit their plans to God during the time of prayer.

Study 11. Galatians 6:11-18. Getting Motivated.

Purpose: To reflect on our primary motives and goals in life.

Verse 11. Various suggestions have been made concerning the "large letters" of verse 11. Some commentators believe that Paul had bad eyesight and refer to Galatians 4:13-15 for support. Others believe that his writing was large (and sloppy?) because he was not a professional scribe. However, given the urgent nature of his letter, the idea of emphasis seems most plausible.

Question 4. Encourage the group to think of specific areas and relationships in their lives, such as their relationships at work or school, with non-Christian friends or neighbors, or with those in their own families who don't know Christ.

Questions 5-6. F. F. Bruce writes, "It is difficult, after sixteen centuries and more during which the cross has been a sacred symbol, to realize the unspeakable horror and loathing which the very mention or thought of the cross provoked in Paul's day" (*The Epistle to the Galatians,* The New International Greek Commentary [Grand Rapids, Mich.: Eerdmans, 1982], p. 271).

If the group has difficulty answering these questions, ask, "How does Paul's attitude toward boasting differ from the world's attitude?" People in "the world" (non-Christian society) boast in their own accomplishments in order to gain the respect and admiration of others. Paul has put to death ("crucified") this kind of attitude. He boasts in Christ not himself. He seeks Christ's approval not the world's. Because of Paul's attitudes the world persecutes him and would crucify him if they could.

Questions 9-10. "The Greek word for 'marks' is *stigmata.* Medieval churchmen believed that these were the scars in the hands, feet and side of Jesus, and that Paul by sympathetic identification with Him found the same scars appearing in his body. . . . It is most unlikely, however, that the *stigmata* of Jesus which Paul bore on his body were of this kind. Doubtless they were rather wounds which he had received while being persecuted for Jesus' sake" (Stott, *Message of Galatians,* pp. 181-82). These wounds proved that he was Christ's servant. Paul did not hesitate to preach the cross of Christ, or to do anything for Christ's sake, even if it meant persecution.

Now or Later. You may want to take an extra study session to work through these wrap-up questions. Use this time to celebrate what you have learned and perhaps to begin planning what you will study next.

Question 1. There are a myriad of ideas discussed in Galatians but only a few major themes. Concentrate on these. Try to avoid a lengthy discussion, however, since most of these ideas are touched on elsewhere in this study.

Question 4. For example, any idea of human merit must be excluded from a proper presentation of the gospel and personal boasting must be excluded from any proper response.

Question 5. This statement comes from Robert H. Schuller, *Self-Esteem: The New Reformation* (Waco, Tex.: Word Books, 1982), p. 39. The question is designed to call to mind and apply Paul's statements about his God-given authority and the source of his message (Gal 1—2).

Question 6. You may be surprised to find that some members of your group will believe that this is a perverted statement of the gospel while others will not. If necessary, ask them to consider how this statement of the gospel differs from that of Paul's opponents. They would probably have affirmed the following: (a) I must believe in Jesus Christ and thereby receive the forgiveness he offers through his death on the cross; (b) I must be circumcised; (c) I must seek to obey the law of God (with the help of the Spirit of God). Are points b and c different in principle from b and c in question 6 on page 45?

Question 7. This question could result in a heated discussion. It is important that the members of your group truly listen to each other, and that they respect each other's differences.

Question 8. Remember, the question is not whether the members of your group are personally for or against such practices. It concerns whether rules such as these, as critics claim, place too little confidence in the Spirit's ability to regulate a Christian's behavior.

Jack Kuhatschek was formerly an executive vice president and publisher at Baker Publishing Group. He is the author of many Bible study guides including Romans *and* David *in the LifeBuilder Bible Study series, and the books* Applying the Bible *and* The Superman Syndrome.